Front cover:
The castle viewed
From the beach.
I.N.A.H.

Photography:
Enrique Franco Torrijos

First edition in English 1982
© Panorama Editorial, S. A.
Leibnitz 31
México 5. D.F.

Text: Demetrio Sodi M.

Photography:
Enrique Franco Torrijos
Walter Reuter
Manuel Valle

I.N.A.H.

Printed in Mexico
Impreso en México

ISBN 968-38-0054-8 English
ISBN 968-38-0053-X Spanish
ISBN 968-38-0055-6 French
ISBN 968-38-0056-4 German.

TULUM

 PANORAMA EDITORIAL, S.A.

How to visit Tulum

The entrance to the site from the car park lies on the western side and the following route is suggested as being the most convenient and complete:

Follow the path leading to the House of the Chultun (structure 20) and to the Temple of the Frescos (structure 16), continue to the House of Columns (structure 21) and then enter the Inner Precinct. From the summit of the incline leading up to the Castle, the visitor has a beautiful panoramic view of both the sea and all the buildings grouped inside the Great Wall.

One of two alternative routes may now be followed.

Either leave the Inner Precinct through the archway situated between structure 9 and 10 to view the platforms linked to Temple 54, or continue in a northerly direction towards the beach, the Temple of the Wind (structure 45), the House of the Cenote (structure 35) and the House of the North East (structure 34). The visitor may then approach the Guard Tower (structure 55) or the House of Halach Uinik (structure 25). This route takes the visitor almost back to the starting point.

Index

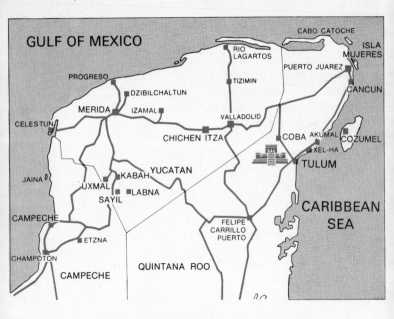

Geographical Location

The archaeological site of Tulum is situated of the coast of the State of Quintana Roo, part of the Yucatan Peninsula, the shores of which are washed by the waters of the Caribbean.

Tulum lies some 450 kilometres from Merida, the capital of the State of Yucatan, and 230 kilometres from the city of Chetumal which is the capital of the State of Quintana Roo. The journey by car or bus from Merida has the added advantage of offering the visitor the opportunity of seeing this fascinating region of the Mexican Republic, as well as other archaeological sites such as Chichen Itza and vestiges of the colonial period, among them the old sisal-growing estates. In this way, the visitor also has the chance to observe the daily life of the villages on the way. These are opportunities not to be missed and, of course, an introduction to the beauties of the Caribbean is not the least attraction.

The southward journey from the world renowned tourist centre of Cancun to Tulum covers a distance of 131 kilometres, taking in the beach of Akumal, one of the most imposing in the area, and the magnificent lakes of Xel-Ha.

The Convent of Izamal, on the road between Merida and Cancun, is a gem of colonial art.

The magnificent waters of the Mexican Caribbean have limitless sporting possibilities.

Yucatán peasants drawing water from a well.

Hotel Accommodation

Cancun is the most practical base for a visit to Tulum, both on account of its comprehensive range of accomodation and tourist services and of its proximity to Puerto Juarez and Puerto Morelos from which ferries leave to Isla Mujeres and Cozumel respectively. The town also enjoys excellent air connections with Mexico City and other parts of the world.

Since the entire archaeological site may be visited in a few hours visitors may, if they wish, return to their hotels in Cancun for the night. Alternatively, there are limited hotel services in Tulum itself, while first class hotel facilities are offered at the beautiful beach of Akumal which is nearer Tulum than Cancun.

Visiting Hours and Special Passes

The archaeological site is open from 8 am. to 5 p.m.; these time may vary according to the season.

Photographs may only be taken outside, without the use of a tripod and for non-commercial ends. A special permit must be

*Dusk on the beautiful
beach of Akumal.*

obtained from the Instituto Nacional de Antropología e Historia
(Cordoba No 45, México City) for the use of more sophisticated
photographic and cinematographic equipment involving the use
of tripods, winches, artificial lighting, cinema cameras, etc.

Passes may be obtained from the same Institute to remain on
the site during the night or to visit before official opening hours.

General Information

The services of guides who show the visitors around and explain
the monuments and history may be obtained on the site itself or
arranged beforehand in tourist agencies in the cities of Merida
and Cancun.

Charges for such services are controlled by the Ministry of
Tourism and depend on the length of the tour.

Since Tulum is situated in a tropical area, the climate is typical
of such regions: on occasions it rains heavily during the summer
months but one may expect hot sun throughout the year.

GENERAL INFORMATION

The famous tourist centre of Cancun lies only 131 kms. from the archaeological site.

THE MAYAS

History

The vast expanse of territory which fell under the influence of the Maya Culture in Mesoamerica covers some 325,000 square kilometres and includes the Mexican States of Yucatan, Campeche, Quintana Roo, Tabasco and the eastern area of Chiapas, as well as the greater part of Guatemala (with the exception of the Pacific coastal belt), Belize and the western regions of Honduras and El Salvador.

The Mayan race was made up of several different groups with similar ethnic characteristics and physical features who were heirs to the same culture. There were, however, differences between the various regions. One of the most notable was that of language variations, even those arising from the same linguistic root. Today, some twenty-four different languages are still spoken in the region, all of Mayan origin.

The Mayas settled in the area in much the same way as did all prehispanic cultures. They built ceremonial centres which were permanently inhabited by the clergy and the nobility whose palaces stood side by side in the ceremonial precincts. Recent exploration and archaeological studies have revealed details on the life style of the upper classes in the Mayan cities although, as yet, little is known of how the subjugated classes, such as the peasants, lived and supported the powerful minority. Broadly speaking, the chronology of the Mayan Culture followed the lines traced by the chronology of Mesoamerica as a whole. Nevertheless, the different time periods of the former may be more clearly defined due, to a certain extent, to the fact that the Mayas dated their steles in accordance with a chronological system, as they did their paintings and ceramics. Their annotations permit us to pin precise historical dates to numerous events as well as to identify the age of materials and objects of different types. According to J. Eric S. Thompson (*Grandeza y decadencia de los mayas*, —Greatness and Fall of the Mayas—, México, Fondo de Cultura

Throne of carved stone. Found in Piedras Negras and currently on exhibition in La Aurora Museum, Guatemala.

13

Detail of a mural in Bonampak, Chiapas. A copy is on display in the National Museum of Anthropology.

Económica, 1959), one of the leading authorities on the Mayan Culture, it may be chronologically classified in the following periods:·

1) *Formative or Preclassic Period*

500 B.C. - 325 A.D. During this period, the budding Mayan tradition was unable to shake off the effects of outside influences, arising principally from the Olmec culture. However, purely Mayan elements were beginning to emerge, among them a ceramic tradition featuring anthropomorphous figures with particular physical features which have since come to be identified with the Mayas. It could be said that these were developed by the ethnic fore-

---

*Sylvanus G. Morley, however, maintains that Mayan history may be divided into three broad periods: 1) Preclassical, approximately 1500 B.C. - 317 A.D; 2) Classical, 317 - 889 A.D.; and 3) Postclassical, 889 - 1697 *(La civilización Maya*-The Mayan Civilization Mexico City, Fondo de Cultura Económica, 1947).

fathers of the present-day Mayas (although the original figures show cranial deformations, a practice which has been dropped by the Mayas of today.) The E-VII-Sub de Uaxactun pyramid in Guatemala is a magnificent example of the persistent influence of other cultures during this period, in that the whole is decorated with distinctly Olmec-type stucco masks.

Their ceramics were of very high quality although there was little variation in design. The two classical styles predominating during this period have been called Mamon and Chicnel, together with the so-called Matzanel sub-style.

Development during the greater part of this period took place principally on the highlands of Guatemala while relatively little progress was made in the lowlands. However, towards the end of the period in question, pyramidal mounds were raised in the Peten and in Yucatan.

2) *Classical Period*

This era spanned the period 325 - 925 A.D. and falls into three phases: Early (325 - 625), Peak (625 - 800) and Decline (800 - 925). During this period, the Mayan Culture reached its apogee and greatest expansion. During the Early Classical Period, the Mayas freed themselves completely from influences exerted by other cultures such as that of the Olmecs. At this point, they began to develop the characteristic features of their own forms of artistic expression.

Hence, the typical Mayan arch was developed and steles erected which recorded both the passing of time and specific historical and mythical events. This activity continued to such an extent that, two centuries after the beginning of the Early Classical Period, many cities could pride themselves on their own local steles and hieroglyphic monuments, This development occurred principally in the highlands of Guatemala, in cities such as Kaminaljuyu, althougt this was a period of stagnation in the lowlands.

The Peak Classical Period followed. This was an era of great expansion in all aspects of life: astronomy, the calendar, hieroglyphic sculpture, architecture, sculpture, ceramics, jewellery-making, characteristic figure decorations, erection of carved steles and the founding of cities. Palenque, Copan, Quirigua, Tikal, Xaxchilan and other magnificent cities were established and grew during this time. Contrary to the Early Period, this renaissance occurred in the lowlands while the highland culture went into decline.

The end of the Classical Period was heralded by the era of the Decline. Many theories have been put forward as to why this decline should have occurred. None is totally convincing, but we will here briefly summarize the most recent, presented again by Eric Thompson.

During this era, the cities were almost totally abandoned (although not altogether as it was believed for many years) and an obvious decadence set in among those who continued to inhabit them. It has been suggested that the city dwellers were forced to emigrate on account of changes in climate or that their lands had been rendered barren by their system of felling, clearing and burning. Another hypothesis is that the lower classes, the peasants, rose up against the nobility and the clergy in response to increasingly heavy taxation and obligatory extra labour for the benefit of the upper classes and for the construction of ceremonial centres.

The latter theory is the most feasible since it has never been proved that any such large scale agricultural problem occurred or that there were any notable changes in climatic conditions. According to Thompson, the peasant uprising was sparked off by some outside influence arising from a Mayan group called the *Putun*, currently known as the *chontal*, who inhabit Tabasco.

From the time of the Classical Period, Nahuatl-speaking groups emigrated from the Central Highlands to the coasts of the Gulf of Mexico and settled in areas bordering on those occupied by the Mayan groups living on its shores. Others travelled as far as the Estuary of the Grijalva River and so became neighbours of the Putun.

The Putun gradually fell under the influence of the Nahuatl culture and came to be at the disposal of the *chontalli* or "foreigner". Hence, the name that they have retained to the present day, in spite of the fact that they were originally Putun. Although the Putun maintained contact with their Mayan relatives, they underwent a process whereby the Nahuatl influence came to predominate over their own Mayan traditions. This resulted in an exotic, hybrid culture which the Putun sought to spread throughout the lowlands.

Their means of achieving this end was closely connected to their way of life since they were, first and foremost, merchants and also sailors. Therefore, they travelled extensively to all the major Mayan cities, crossing swamps and sailing up river against the current, to sell their products. Hence, by necessity of trade, they became highly skilled in the techniques of sailing and navigation.

Moreover, they had laid a road right around the Yucatan Peninsula, reaching as far south as present-day Honduras and they later erected a major sanctuary dedicated to their own goddess Ixchel, on the island of Cozumel. It is also probable that we should attribute to them the extensive Toltec influence which subsequently became apparent in Chichen Itza. This hypothesis resides on the fact that a Nahuatlized Putun group, called the Itza, used the Pole post founded by the Putunes as a resting place on the journey north from what is now Quintana Roo, as their base

*Detail of the hieroglyphics
of the Initial Series; Yaxchilan,
Chiapas. The complete series
of hieroglyphics has been
translated to give the date 526 A.D.*

for founding the Mexican Chichen Itza on the remains of the Classical Period Chichen. The small boat found by Columbus near Cuba must almost certainly have been of Putun manufacture. Their trade endeavours reached even to those far regions.

Hence, the Nahuatlized Putunes took it upon themselves to disseminate new ideas among the peoples of the lowlands, eventually leading to the uprising of the peasants against the upper classes. This brought about an exodus from the cities and ceremonial centres although they were certainly not left totally deserted. Documents relating to the arrival of the Spaniards in the area show that it was highly populated during the sixteenth century, ceremonial centres existed and the populations spoke several different languages. Several chroniclers of the time went so far as to present precise population figures, information on animals and food products and housing and described the rituals conducted in the presence of the horrified Spanish friars.

3) *Interregnum or Transitional Period*

(925-975 A.D.) During this period the region did not suffer total depopulation. Various groups remained and expanded, constituting the bridge between the Decline Period and the period that followed, called by Thompson the *Interregnum*. With the loss of their guides and wise men, of their true scholars of religion and of the calendar, and of their prophets and leaders, the Mayan peasants of the area allowed their culture to degenerate over a period of only fifty years to a level below that reached during the Formative Period. They performed primitive rituals in the almost abandoned cities and buried their former despotic lords with ceremonies and offerings which never equalled the splendour of the Classical Period.

The real fall of the Mayan Culture occurred during the Decline and the Interregnum. Subsequent events were, in fact, no more than the combined effects of the aftermath of the extraordinary Classical Period and of other influences, principally those arising from the Nahuatl Culture of the Toltec Period. Although the Mayas struggled to regain their past glories, they never succeeded.

4) *Mexican or Maya-Toltec Period*

This period, which spans the years 975 -1200 A.D., was best represented in the northern part of the Yucatan Peninsula and especially in Chichen Itza. At this point the Mayan tradition was integrated with that of the Toltecs from the Central Highlands. However, a certain degree of decadence was still apparent and the creativity characteristic of the Classical Period degenerated into a mere effort to copy outside art, especially that of Tula, the Toltec capital. All their buildings, colonnades and relief sculpture were

*The trading routes of the putunes
followed the coastline of
the Yucatan Peninsula down
to Honduras. Detail of a mural
in Chichen Itza. Copy in the
National Anthropological Museum.*

eclectic, although it should be pointed out that, nevertheless, the quality of their reliefs, painting, sculpture and architecture was superior to that executed in Tula. The sensitivity inherited by the Mayan artists and artisans was, in fact, more highy developed than that of the Toltecs.

The characteristics of what might be likened to the European city-states of the same period became more directly apparent and alliances were formed between different cities (or, more accurately, between the major governing families), ensuring mutual support, and seeking to obtain hegemony over the territory and sharing booty gleaned during military ventures.

One of the major alliances of this time was established in 1,000 A.D. between the Xiu family of Uxmal, the Itzaes of Chichen and the Cocom of Mayapan. However, it was betrayed in about 1194 by the leader of the Cocom, Hunac Ceel, who imprisoned the nobles of Xiu and of the Itzaes and had them brought to Mayapan which was turned into a fortified city. It would appear that the captive nobles continued to have a say in government, though through representation only.

5) *Period of Mexican absorption*

This period runs from 1200 - 1540 A.D. during which time Mayapan came to hold complete sway, as occurred with the Quiches in Guatemala during the same period. However, the death knell sounded for both the Quiches and for Mayapan during the fourteenth century when a series of uprisings took place. Hence, in 1412, a Xiu chieftain from Uxmal called Ah Xupan Xiu, destroyed Mayapan with the backing of other leaders. All the cocomes were massacred with the exception of a single prince who was absent from the city on a trading expedition to Honduras. The Quiches, for their part, divided into small groups under different leaders who were continually at war until the conquest of 1525.

Immediately after this massacre, the Mayas decided that they wished to readopt their old traditions. However, they only succeeded in so far as reinstating their own language in preference to the Nahuatl language. It appears that throughout the period of Putun influence and Nahuatl domination, the Mayas never ceased to be bilingual. A prime example is the famous doña Marina or Malintzín (more commonly called the Malinche) who proved to be so useful to Cortes as interpreter on account of her knowledge of both the Mayan and Nahuatl languages. Her knowledge of both languages may be attributed to the fact that she was native of a Nahuatlized Mayan area of present-day Tabasco.

War, the practice of human sacrifice which had become increasingly common under the Nahuatl influence, and the principal worship of Quetzalcoatl-Kukulcan were never completely suppressed or abolished. It was this tarnished image of the splendours achieved by the Mayas of the Classical Period that met the eyes of the Spaniards in 1519, when Cortes disembarked on the island of Cozumel.

In 1541, Francisco de Montejo conquered T'Ho, on the ruins of which he raised the city of Merida, currently the capital of the state of Yucatan. Meanwhile, the Putun stood fast and preserved their independence in their capital city, Acalan, until 1695. The Itzaes who had been driven from Chichen Itza after Hunac Heel's betrayal settled in Guatemala in their last capital which bore the name Tayasal, standing on the shores of the Chankanab Lake which is today called Peten Itza. Here they nurtured the Mayan tradition until 1697 when they were finally defeated by the conquistadors.

Female figure in clay,
Jaina, Campeche.

Architecture

The beginnings of an individual architectural style were already to be seen during the Formative Period when the Mayan Culture had not yet shaken off outside influences, and continued to develop until about the year 900 A.D. This finding is borne out by a monument discovered in Uaxactun, to the north of Tika, which was the largest city of the Mayan civilization. This monument has been given the name E-VII sub, of the E group in that city. In typical Mayan style, this building was covered by another pyramid. Since the outer construction had been destroyed, archaeolgists decided to remove it completely, revealing the older, inner core, in other words, the "sub".

The sub is a quadrangular-based construction with superimposed terraces. A stairway of sophisticated design, bordered with struts bearing jaguar masks, runs up either side. It is conjectured that the jaguar was the god of rain. This building certainly betrays a purely Olmec influence. At this stage, it would be most accurate to speak of an exclusively tributary artistic style. The whole of the sub was covered with a layer of polished stucco, serving as a platform for a temple which no longer exists. However, the holes into which the temple's supporting columns were sunk are still visible, making it possible to reconstruct the whole as it was originally.

Although the Mayan arch, which was developed during the Classical Period, was the most characteristic feature of their architecture, various other elements (mouldings, columns, cresting and superimposed terraces) combined to constitute different Mayan architectural styles, of which the following are the most important:

1) *The Petén Style*

The buildings were erected on superimposed terraces, with connecting stairways projecting from the facade. The decorative element was most frequently composed of stucco masks. There were relatively few openings in the outer shell of the construction, resulting in thick walls and narrow rooms. The wall behind the temples was decorated with large-scale cresting and the facades with stucco relief, etc. This style predominates in cities such as Uaxactun, Tikal, Piedras Negras, Nakum and Calamul.

The Castle seen from the Temple of Warriors, Chichen Itza, Yucatan.

Part of the Nuns' Quadrangle with the Temple of Venus, Uxmal, Yucatan.

Walled arch. Governor's Palace, Uxmal, Yucatan.

2) *Palenque Style*

Vertical bases; stairways bounded by struts; two room temples, the second being the sanctuary; cresting on the central wall; facades bearing friezes running parallel to the arches and decorated with stucco figures; more openings than solid wall space. Most frequent in cities such as Palenque, Tonina, Copan, Quirigua, Yaxchilan and Bonampak.

3 *The Rio Bec Style*

Primarily ornamental, apparent in the stylization of the pyramid bases and simulated stairways and towers. Stone mosaic used, as in Xpuhil, Rio Bec and Hormiguero.

4) *Chenes Style*

Graduated sloping bases; open spaces cut by columns and vertical friezes; cresting on the front of buildings; highly complex decoration featuring picturesque scenes and using ornamental panels, lattice work, small drums and columns, large masks of the

*Temple of the Sun,
Palenque, Chiapas.*

rain god represented in mosaic of cut and arranged stone. Typical of cities such as Hochob, Edzna, Xcalumkin, Sayil, Labna, Chacmultun and Uxmal.

5) *The Puuc Style*

Similar to the Chenes style, except that decoration is restricted to the friezes, using mosaic of carefully cut, carved and arranged stone, as opposed to covering the entire facade. Abounds in Chichen Itza.

6) *The Mexican Style*

Product of the Toltec influence in the northern Mayan region although it also contains elements of the Puuc style. Bases or platforms with high taluses bearnig panels or cornices; stairways decorated with serpent heads at the base of the bordering struts; altars adorned with skulls; columns in serpent form. To be found in cities such as Chichen Itza, Tulum, Mayapan, Coba, Acanceh and other parts of Yucatan and Quintana Roo.

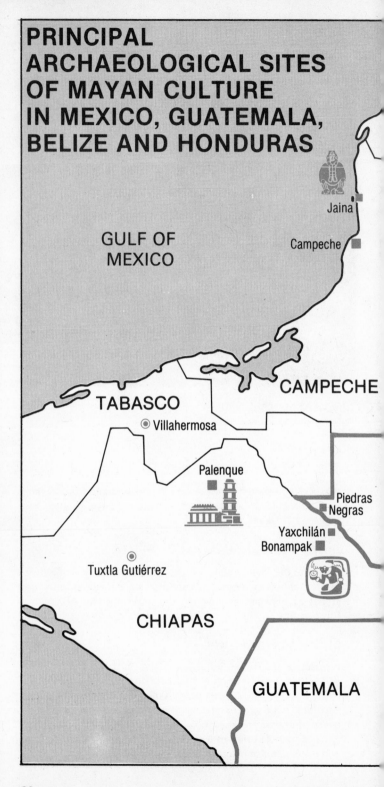

PRINCIPAL ARCHAEOLOGICAL SITES OF MAYAN CULTURE IN MEXICO, GUATEMALA, BELIZE AND HONDURAS

Jaina

Campeche

GULF OF MEXICO

CAMPECHE

TABASCO

◉ Villahermosa

Palenque

Piedras Negras

Yaxchilán

Bonampak

◉ Tuxtla Gutiérrez

CHIAPAS

GUATEMALA

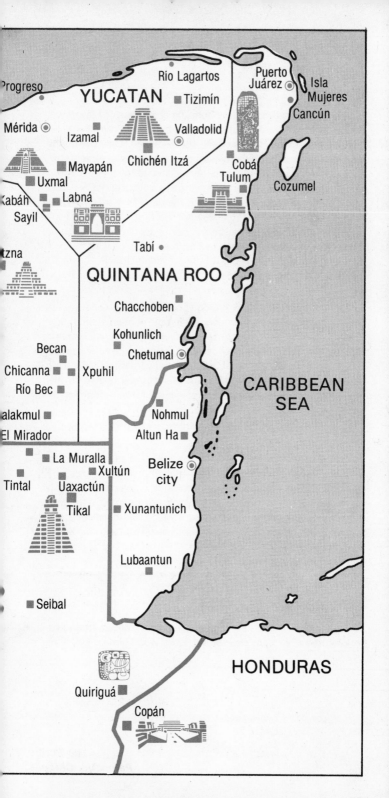

Progreso

YUCATAN
Río Lagartos
Tizimín
Puerto Juárez
Isla Mujeres
Cancún

Mérida
Izamal
Valladolid

Chichén Itzá
Mayapán
Uxmal
Kabáh
Labná
Sayil
Cobá
Tulum
Cozumel

tzna
Tabí

QUINTANA ROO

Chacchoben

Kohunlich
Becan
Chetumal
Chicanna
Xpuhil
Río Bec
alakmul
El Mirador

CARIBBEAN SEA

Nohmul
La Muralla
Altun Ha
Xultún
Belize city
Tintal
Uaxactún
Tikal
Xunantunich

Lubaantun

Seibal

HONDURAS

Quiriguá
Copán

Writing

Is was for a long time believed that the characters of Mayan writing could be interpreted phonetically. However, this hypothesis has not as yet been satisfactorily substantiated. Only the mathematical and chronological hieroglyphics have been successfully deciphered. It has, for example, been demostrated that the Mayas had basic ideogrammes or arithmetic symbols: the dot ● which had a numerical value of 1, the unit, the dash ▬ with a numerical value of 5, and a stylized shell ⬭ symbolizing 0. These elements served as the basis of a vigesimal system from 0 to 19 in which the signs were attributed a relative value in accordance with the position in which they were placed. This system, together with the use of 0, was used by the Mayas centuries before it was discovered by any other culture in the world.

The chronological-type hieroglyphs used by the Mayas demonstrate their interest in understanding the phenomenon of time. Their knowledge of astronomy was such that they were able to develop humanity's best-ever calendar, namely, the solar calendar (called HAAB), consisting of 365 days and a fraction, divided into eighteen months of twenty days each - thereby related to their system of mathematical calculation - and a further month of five days completing the annual cycle.

Each day and each month had a different name related to their deities.

They also had a second calendar for ritual purposes (called TZOLK'IN), consisting of 260 days spanning twenty cycles of 13 days each. The days were given the same names as in the solar calendar while the thirteen day cycles were named differently. The Mayas established a starting date for both calendars on which to base their reckoning of the years. This date was known as 4 AHAU (ritual), 8 CUMKU (solar) which has been calculated to correspond to the year 3113 B.C.

Sculpture and Ceramics

These were the most outstanding elements of Mayan art and were executed in stucco, clay, stone, jade, wood and precious metals.

The Scribe,
Palenque, Chiapas.

Mayan ceremonial dish.
From Lagartero, Chiapas.
National Anthropological Museum.

They carved steles, panels, lintels, facades, door jambs and window posts, columns, stairways, etc.

Their masks and sculptures portrayed human figures, gods, priests, atlantes, etc. Their works in high and low relief as well as their ceramics were designed for both religious and everyday use and were all of extraordinary artistic quality. Many pieces of sculpture and ceramic work were given a polychrome finish.

Painting

This was principally decorative although some paintings had a religious, ritual or historical significance. Painting was also used in fresco work to represent mythological or religious scenes or in a more descriptive, realistic, narrative form to represent scenes of war, landscapes, animals or customs. Paintings were also executed on codices, ceramics, stuccos, columns and facades.

TULUM

History of Tulum

A series of archaeological sites are to be found along the entire eastern coast of the Yucatan Peninsula. Most are very similar to Tulum and date likewise from a relatively late period during the centuries immediately preceding the Spanish Conquest. A few however, unlike Tulum, show indications of greater antiquity and contain steles engraved with hieroglyphics reaching as far back as the sixth century A.D. Ichpaatun is a prime example.

Nevertheless, Tulum is the major centre along that coast where many of the remaining sites have not been extensively explored nor efforts made to conserve them. These sites are, from north to south: El Meco, Nisucte, Playa del Carmen, Palmul, Acomal (Acumal), Xelha, Toncah, Tulum, Xcaret, Cacakal, Punta Soliman, Chacmol, Canche Balam, Ichpaatun and others in the bay of Chetumal.

Archaeological sites also exist on the islands along this coast such as, for example, Isla Mujeres and Cancun, the latter having recently been joined to the mainland. However, the major island sites are situated on Cozumel. To date, twelve individual sites have been discovered, the major ones being El Real, Punta Molas, Celarain, San Gervasio, San Severo, San Benito, El Cedral and Cinco Puertas.

This was the biding place of Geronimo de Aguilar and Gonzalo Guerrero, the two Spaniards who survived a shipwreck while on an expedition which set out from the Darien in 1511. They had lived on Cozumel for eight years when Cortes landed there and learned of their existence. Cortes invited them to join him in the Conquest though only the friar Aguilar accepted. His knowledge of the Mayan language allowed him to render great service to Cortes as interpreter. Aguilar and Malintzin (the Malinche) were able to converse with the Aztec authorities as well as with other peoples conquered by the Spaniards. Guerrero declined the invitation on the grounds that he was married to a Mayan woman of noble origins and had had children by her. At the time of the battles waged against the Spaniards a few years later, Guerrero fought with the Mayas against his former countrymen.

In the book *Las Relaciones de Yucatan* (Events in the Yucatan)
written by the Spaniards years after the Conquest, the city of Zama was described as a walled enclave containing stone bulidings
of which one was exceptionally large, the whole having the appear-
ance of a fortress. Its approximate location is also given, further
supporting the hypothesis that the place currently known as Tulum is none other than the ancient city of Zama. The translation
of the place name as "dawn" is fully justified if we consider that it
faces east where the sun rises.

On the same subject, the chronicler Pedro Sanchez de Aguilar
states in his work *Informe contra Idolorum Cultores del Obispo de
Yucatan*: *"Let it be understood that when the cacique Kenich
captured the ten Spaniards who were washed up on the shores of
Zama when their ship was wrecked, he described to them his war
strategems which were the same as those later employed by the
Cupul people against the Conquistadors. Among the ten Spanish
captives was Geronimo de Aguilar, native of Ecija and of noble
blood, who fought for his new master in several wars; his tongue
won Mexico. It was Aguilar who found Cortes on Cozumel where
he ordered that a cross be erected and decorated when he set out
for Mexico with his fleet which he had wrested from the control
of the Govenor don Diego Fernandez de Velasco in 1604 and later
sent to the Marques del Valle, Cortes' grandson"*. This was written by Sanchez de Aguilar in the seventeenth century, the book
being published in Madrid in 1639. However, another historian
who also wrote in the seventeenth century, the Franciscan monk
Diego Lopez de Cogolludo, claims that the two Spaniards were
found further south, on Cape Catoche. He states in his history of
Yucatan that Cortes gave the Indians letters, glass beads and
other goods as ransom since Aguilar had become a cacique's sla-
ve and, as we have already seen, he fought with his master's tro-
ops against other Mayan groups. In the words of Cogolludo:

*"The Indians who had been entrusted with General Cortes' let-
ter, delivered it a few days later to a Spaniard by the name of Geronimo de Aguilar. Some say that the Indians dared not deliver
the letter to him directly but preferred to give it to his master.
Aguilar was most unsure that he would be permitted to leave and
so, with great humility, he told his master that he left the decision
entirely in his hands as was his wont in all matters, which explains
how he had survived. His master not only permitted him to leave
but also sent some Indians along to accompany him, begging
Aguilar to solicit the friendship of the Spaniards for his people
since the Spaniards were such valiant men"*. However, Bernal
Diaz writes: *"The ransom and letter was given to Geronimo de
Aguilar who was overjoyed and went to his master bearing the
letter and ransom to seek his permission to leave, which was immediately granted, by which Aguilar was much gratified. Having
thus obtained his master's permission, Geronimo de Aguilar*

Tulum was first seen by European eyes in 1518, during the expedition led by Juan de Grijalba.

sought the other Spaniard called Gonzalo Guerrero and showed him the letter and explained to him what had happened. Guerrero replied: *"Brother Aguilar, I am married and I have three children. I have become cacique of the people here and their chieftain in time of war. My face is tattooed and my ears pierced. What will these Spaniards say to me when they see me in this state? Go with God, since you see how beautiful my children are. But give me those green beads you carry that I might make a present of them to my people and say that my brothers brought them for me from my homeland".*

All seems to indicate that Western eyes first saw Tulum in 1518, a year prior to Cortes' arrival in Cozumel, when Juan de Grijalba's expedition sailed down the eastern coast of the Yucatan Peninsula. The sight of Tulum caused Juan Diaz, author of the expedition's journal, who had seen many coastal settlements, to exclaim: *"it is so large that the city of Seville seems neither larger nor better... like a very high tower".*

No more is heard of Tulum until the nineteenth century but it may be supposed, although it is not known whether the region was inhabited after the Conquest, that it suffered the same fate as other coastal settlements which came into conflict with the Spaniards on several occasions on account of their stubborn refusal to surrender. They must finally have been conquered in 1544, by which time the whole of the Yucatan Peninsula had fallen under Spanish dominion. Throughout the sixteenth and seventeenth centuries, Tulum was continually attacked by English, French and Dutch pirates.

During the bloody Caste War of 1847, an Indian uprising which was brutally suppressed by the Government forces, Tulum was occupied on several occasions by the rebel Indians who sought the relative protection of its fortified walls. In 1871, in the course of another war, Tulum became a sacred place of the Indians, containing a "Talking" or "Miraculous Cross" which responded to the powers of an Indian woman called Maria Uicab who was known as the holy patron or queen of Tulum. The enormous influx of tourists during the sixties put an end to its function as a holy shrine.

It was the eastern coast which was most seriously affected by the war. The Tulum region later became a major gum producing centre but when the industry went into decline with the invention of synthetic gum, the emphasis was placed on fishing and coconut production as may be seen along the entire eastern coast today.

The Archaeology of the Eastern Coast of the Yucatan peninsula

In a report published in 1946, Escalona Ramos listed 36 archaeological sites located between the Bay of Chetumal and the northern-most point of the state of Quintana Roo, including the island of Cozumel. On the other hand, the reports compiled by Lizardi and Fernandez deal mainly with the sites of Mario Ancona, Las Higueras and Las Moras. Steles of very ancient origin have been discovered at certain sites such as Ichpaatun, findings here dating from 564 A.D, which was the height of the Classical Period. Stele I at Tulum dates from the same period, and is considered by some to mark the founding of the city. However, this hypothesis is discounted by the fact that all the buildings are of more recent construction. The presence of the ancient stele at this site is easily accounted for by the fact that the Mayas customarily transported steles and other objects from long-abandoned cities to their new settlements. During the 1920s, Thomas Gann carried this stele back to London where it is to this day on exhibition in the British Museum.

The first buildings in Tulum must have been erected towards the end of the XII century, while its major development occurred during the XIII and beginning of the XIV century.

The Temple of the Frescos is a particularly clear example of the practice of erecting an initial building of one style and covering it with other structures of a completely different style. The superimposed structure used wood rather than domes, with rectangular bays entered through porticos of columns with capitals. In their simplest form, the bays were roofed with tree trunks resting on the walls. However, in some instances, they were divided by a

*This is how Tulum was seen by
the English artist and archaeologist,
Frederick Catherwood, in 1842.*

central row of columns along which ran a beam serving as a central point of support for the roof, the outer walls supporting the roof on either side.

The friezes, whose importance resides in the fact that they were the chief form of decoration in this ancient site, were integrated into the buildings by raising the columns on small stone pillars. The wooden architrave was then slotted into place. It is possible that this type of roofing may later have been employed in combination with the dome since, in certain cases, both the original and the superimposed structure use this method, as may be seen in the Temple of the Frescos and in the Castle of Tulum. The outward slope of the wall is much exaggerated in these two buildings. Even the door jambs are sloping or trapezoidal, narrowing towards the top. Althougt the use of panels featuring the Descending God is not exclusive to Tulum, it is certainly more common here than anywere else, as seen in the Temple of the Frescos and in Temple V.

Certain structures, such as those in the upper section of the Castle, continued to use the columns which are typical of the region. However, in this particular case, a clear Toltec influence is detectable in the rattlesnake designs added to the columns as capitals, carved heads of these same snakes serving as pedestals. However, unlike in other sites such as Chichen Itza, the features of the bird snake are painted rather than carved.

Archaeological Expeditions and Studies in Tulum

According to a letter penned by Juan Pio Perez in 1840, Tulum was rediscovered in that year by Juan José Galvez. However, the fame of the place was spread throughout the world by John Lloyd Stephens, the American explorer. He was accompanied on his travels by an Englishman, of outstanding drawing ability, named Frederick Catherwood, the first man ever to reproduce a precise copy of the Mayan epigraphy. These were published in his book *Incidents of Travel in Central America, Chiapas and Yucatan*. The book appeared in 1848, six years after their first visit to the site.

In 1895, the explorer W.H. Holmes made two drawings of the buildings. These drawings were, however, long distance views executed from a boat for fear of the Indians who were still up in arms in the War of Castes. The first truly scientific research of the site was undertaken between 1916 and 1922 by the Washington Carnegie Institute. Howe, Sylvanus Morely and Prince William of Sweden participated in this work. The results of their research, together with the first scientific map made of the city, were publicized by Samuel K. Lothrop in his magnificent work *An archaeological Study of the East Coast of Yucatan*, published in 1924.

The monuments of the Eastern region are registered, though somewhat inaccuately, in the *Archaeological Atlas of the Mexican Republic* (INAH) and in 1937 a Mexican Scientific Expedition was sent to study Tulum and many other archaeological sites of the Eastern coast. This expedition also registered previously undocumented ruins further into the interior of the peninsula. A section of the expedition's final report was published by Alberto Escalona Ramos in *El Boletín de la Sociedad Mexicana de Geografía y Estadística* (Newsletter of the Mexican Geographical and Statistical Society) - Volume LXI, No. 3, 1946. A further section was published by the archaeologist Miguel Angel Fernandez in *Anales del Museo Nacional de Arqueología* (*Annals of the National Archaeological Museum*) - Volume III, Stage V, 1945. Information on the facts compiled during this expedition was completed by Cesar Lizardi Ramos in his booklet entitled *Exploraciones en Quintana Roo* (Explorations in Quintana Roo).

The exploratory work begun in Tulum by Miguel Angel Fernandez in 1938 was of several years duration. His work was not only of an exploratory nature; he also took upon himself the task of conservation and restoration of the ancient site, as commissioned by the National Anthropological and Historical Institute. In 1954, William T. Sanders of the Carnegie Institute carried out a study of the ceramic work found along the Eastern Coast, including that of Tulum.

Finally, The South-Eastern Regional Centre of the INAH dispatched archaeologists, restorers and topographers to work at the site between 1974-75. The results of their work are to be seen not only within the walled city itself but also in its immediate surroundings.

The Meaning of the Name Tulum

Tulum, the modern name of this archaeological site, means fence, fortified wall, trench, stockade. It was given this name on account of the fortified wall which ran around three sides of the city on the north, south and west. The remaining eastern flank was defended by the rock face rising from the waters of the Caribbean. However, everything seems to indicate that in ancient times it was called Zama, which has been translated as "dawn".

Tulum and its Buildings

The buildings, tombs and platforms that are visible today within the walled city constitute only a small part of Tulum in its original form. In fact, the remains of this settlement spread along the coast

Panoramic view of Tulum.

for some six kilometres, 90% consisting of large, densely populated sections to the north and south of the walled section. Only the latter section is on public view today but constitutes a mere 10% of the original city. No complete study or recostruction has been made of the habitational areas of the city although preliminary research has uncovered streets, patios and platforms of dwellings. Grinding stones have been found and shrines and buildings of the distinctive Mayan architectural style uncovered. Several springs and cenotes providing the city with drinking water have also been located.

These settlements display no clearly-defined urban planning model. Ecological features dictated the nature of these settlements, in contrast to Teotihuacan or Monte Alban. Tulum simply spread north and south, taking advantage of natural features, until it was brought short by the Caribbean in the East and by mangrove swamps in the West. The dwellings were built either of stone work or of perishable materials such as wood, straw or palm leaves, depending on the social standing of the citizen.

The major buildings of Tulum are grouped within the walled precinct which consists of a huge rectangular space bordered by the

*Reconstruction of Tulum
by Lothrop.*

immense wall which is six metres thick and measures between three and five metres high. The area within the wall measures 380 metres from north to south and 170 metres from east to west. As we have already seen, the eastern side of the city is flanked by the sea and also by a beautiful beach lying to the north of the major buildings. Not all the buildings within the precinct were designed for purely religious purposes, such as shrines and tombs; some served as dwellings and others as centres of political and administrative activities.

A group of buildings surrounding a central square within the Great Wall or Outer Precinct constitute the Inner Precinct which is also rectangular in shape and measures fifty by thirty metres. The city's major buildings are grouped within the Inner Precinct and are numbered 1-12 on the plan. In fact, many of the city's buildings have been destroyed with time while others have survived with surprisingly little damage. In the above-mentioned book by Stephens and Catherwood, it is apparent that buildings which were in good repair at the time book appeared have since lost walls and roofs. Hence, we will discuss only the major, best preserved buildings and those which are of particular interest.

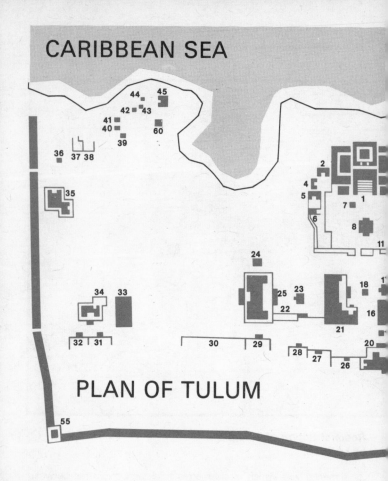

CARIBBEAN SEA

PLAN OF TULUM

The Castle **1**

Temple of the Frescos **16**

House of Halach Uinik **25**

Temple of the Descending God **5**

House of the Chultun **20**

Temple of the Initial series **9**

Mouse of Columns **21**

House of the Cenote **35**

Tombs **13, 14** and **19**

Guard Towers **55, 56**

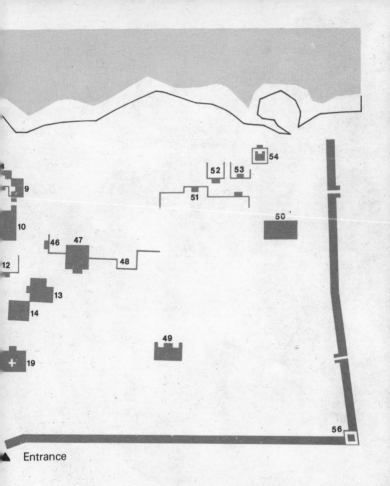

Entrance

Temple of the Wind **45**

Temple of the Sea **54**

Platform of the Conches **66**

House of the Northwest **34**

Ceremonial Platforms **8, 17**

Shrines **15, 18, 24, and 36**

Habitational Platforms **26, 27, 28, 29, 30, 31, 32, 33, 37, 38, 46, 47, 48, 49, 50, 51, 52 and 53.**

Other structures, temples, shrines and platforms **2, 3, 4, 6, 7, 10, 11, 12, 22, 23, 26, 32, 39, 40, 41, 42, 43, and 44.**

The Great Wall or Outer Precinct

The wall was constructed, on the one hand, for defensive purposes and, on the other, to contain those buildings of a political or religious nature.

Its shape and measurements have already been described. At this point it should simply be added that it has five narrow entrances; two to the north, the most easterly of which is flanked by two small rooms within the wall; two on the southern side and one on the western side. Since the car park has been built near this entrance, it is the one most regularly used by visitors. Two small temples (structures 55 and 56) are located in the north-eastern

*The south entrance in
the Great Wall.*

and south-eastern angles of the wall and these may also have served as guard towers.

Unprotected spaces of some twelve metres in width appear at the extreme northern and southern ends of the wall, leaving a curious weak spot in the defence of the area.

The Great Wall was restored and strengthened in 1974-75 by the South-East Regional Centre of the INAH. It should be pointed out that Tulum is not the only walled city to be found along the eastern coast. An example is Xelha, and we should not forget the walled precinct in the city of Chacchoh and the immense wall surrounding Mayapan.

The Inner Precinct

The major buildings are located in this area which must have constituted the heart of the city. There is an overall feeling of balance between these buildings although they are all of varying shape and size and are not symetrically arranged. The principal buildings are the Castle (structure 1); the Temple of the Descending God (structure 5) and the Temple of the Initial Series (structure 9). The remaining buildings within the Inner Precinct may be divided into three types. Structures 2, 3, 4, 10 and 11 are temples; structures 6 and 7 are shrines and structure 8 may have been a platform used for dances and other such purposes.

The temples within the Inner Precinct are all similar with the exception of structure 4 which has a small sanctuary and structures

*The Inner Precinct with
its major buildings.*

3 and 10 which contain interior columns combining to form a portico in the latter. The difference between the temples and the shrines lies in the fact that the latter are lower constructions which has given rise to the belief that the inhabitants of the eastern coast must have been of small stature. Dance platforms such as structure 8 having stairway access on two sides, were a common architectural feature throughout the Mayan area. A low wall runs between most of the buildings although the Precinct may be entered at some points through the spaces between certain buildings which leads one to suppose that the wall served to divide the Inner Precinct from the rest of the city, combining all the major buildings in a single complex, rather than for defensive purposes.

The Castle
(structure 1)

The form of the Castle as it is to be seen today is the product of at least three different periods of construction. It is the highest construction in the city and it must certainly have been this building which the Spaniards of the Grijalba expedition assumed to be a tower. The city as a whole, as seen from the sea, was considered by these men to be superior even to Seville. It is located at the extreme eastern end of the ceremonial centre. Its highest point is the rear facade which is supported by an immense, sloping buttress linked to the structure as a whole at the extreme edge of the stonework which rises some twelve metres above the waters of the Caribbean which wash the rocks below, sloping and then rising gently rowars the west.

The Castle.

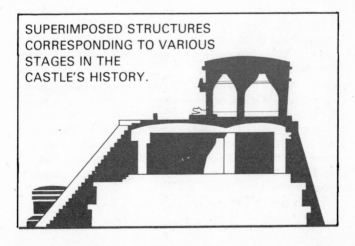

SUPERIMPOSED STRUCTURES
CORRESPONDING TO VARIOUS
STAGES IN THE
CASTLE'S HISTORY.

The northern and southern ends of the building are the only points at which the oldest part of the construction is visible since the central part of the original building was hidden from sight when the structures of the second phase were erected. However, it may be deduced that, during the first phace, the buildings consisted of a double gallery or twin corridors over a terrace of gently sloping walls which was entered by means of a stairway with a central strut. The narrow inner gallery opened at three points into the outer one which was more spacious on account of a central row of columns supporting a flat roof of beams and chalk-based concrete.

The whole of the central part of these galleries was filled in during the second phase of construction. The stairway built during the first phase was prolonged to join up with the tear facade of the sloping wall which served as a buttres. A narrow corridor was built on top of the central section which had been filled in, allowing movement between the northern and southern sections of the building. Painted figures have been discovered on the different layers of stucco covering the eastern wall.

The temple of the second phase, built on top of the filled-in area of the original structure, featuring the new stairway and the

The entrances to the temple adjoining the Castle
are composed of columns in the form of snakes
whose heads form the base of the pillars and whose
tails support the lintel above the entrance.

The remains of a human figurine
are to be seen in one of the
recesses decorating the front
of the upper temple of the Castle.

Decoration on the upper part of the corners of the Castle.

RECONSTRUCTION OF THE CASTLE
(by Lothrop)

buttress, consisted of two corridors which served as sanctuary and portico. The entrance-way was composed of three openings divided by a pair of columns in snake form, their rattle tails supporting the lintel and their heads stretching down to the base. The columns still bear the traces of painted plumage. As is frequent in Tulum, the walls of the building slope outwards while the door jambs slope inwards.

The frieze is very simple, consisting of two bands which extend beyond the upper ends of the columns, forming three recesses. The central recess, although partially destroyed, depicts the Descending God; the northern recess exhibits the remains of a standing figure which may have been repeated in the southern recess, of which nothing remains today. In the corners of the main, west-facing facade, plumed masks may be seen. The portico and sanctuary contain benches and the dome resembles a transversally cut bottle, a common feature of the architecture of Tulum.

Finally, during the third period of construction, two small rooms or shrines were built onto what remained of the facade built during the first phase. The northern-most room was roofed with beams while the second had a domed roof.

*The Temple of Frescos
is the most interesting
building in Tulum,.*

Temple of the Frescos
(structure 16)

Although this is not the most important building, from the archaeological point of view of the information it provides on the cos-
movision of the Mayas, it is, nonetheless, the most interesting in
this ceremonial centre. It is situated at the central point of the
city, to the west of the Inner Precinct and to the east of the main
street. Like all the other buildings in Tulum, it is the end result of a
series of different phases of construction. It began as a single,
low chamber with a domed roof curving inwards from the floor.
The entrance was situated on the western side and a small altar
stood at one end.

Later, a gallery was built around the structure on the north,
west and south sides and four columns with rectangular capitals
were integrated into the western-facing entrance. This structure
was strengthened during a third building phase so as to allow
another temple to be built on top of it. A retaining wall was built

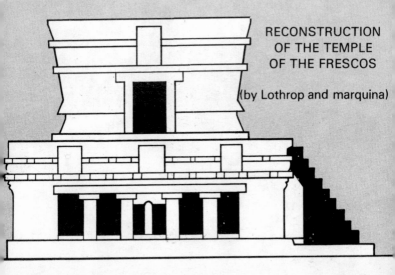

RECONSTRUCTION
OF THE TEMPLE
OF THE FRESCOS

(by Lothrop and marquina)

55

behind it (to the east), partially covering a platform belonging to the original temple. A square column was built in the centre of the access and a buttress on either side. The extreme eastern end of the north corridor was filled with stones to support the roof.

The mural paintings are best conserved in the first temple due to the fact that they were protected by the superimposed gallery and they have also undergone extensive restoration work. The facade is decorated with a double panel bearing human figures, rosettes and interlacing spirals in painted stucco. The western facade bears a frieze which is interrupted above the entrance by three recesses. The central recess contains a depiction of the Descending God while those on either side show figures bearing plumed headdresses. the sunken architrave panel is decorated with impressions of human hands in red. Stucco rosettes decorate the mouldings of the facade and, between the recesses and the panels, appear stucco reliefs showing two male figures entwined with a snake or cord or, according to Gutierre Tibon, with their own umbilical cords. The north-eastern and south-eastern corners of the building are adorned with two large stucco masks representing an ancient deity, perhaps Chaac, the god of water or, more likely, Itzamna, the greatest god of the Mayas whose name means, the being who gives life, the sole creator.

Returning to the most ancient temple, the spaces between the panels and the facade itself are covered with mural paintings on a background of black and blue-green, depicting deities, entwined serpents and a range of offerings including flowers, fruits and ears of maize, all of which are related to the fecundity of nature. The representations are symbolic rather than realistic and the influence of the Central Highlands is clearly visible in these paintings.

Finally, the Upper Temple, which dates from the third phase of construction, displays the typical, outward-sloping walls. The mouldings are simple and the central recess contains the remains of a figure that may have represented the Descending God, both elements being common to the architectural style of Tulum. The single chamber contains a small altar at one end and, as usual, the curved dome resembles a neckless bottle.

Stele 2 of Tulum (structure 15) stands opposite the main facade of the Temple of the Frescos on a pedestal or shrine. Its dimensions and style are similar to that of stele 1 but the date it bears has been so worn with time that it is impossible to establish it with any degree of certainty.

One of the masks decorating
the corners of the Temple of the Frescos.

The mural paintings inside the Temple of the Frescos give a symbolic depiction of the fecundity of nature.

House of Halach Uinik
(structure 25)

This building is situated to the north of structure 21 with a large patio lying between them. This patio contains a small central platform (structure 23) and also a much larger platform which links palaces No. 21 and 25. Structure 23 may have been a shrine, containing a small bench which occupies much of the small interior space. It is entered from the north. In the course of explorations of the site, fragments of earthenware were discovered at this spot, and also the remains of incense burners which were very common at that time. Domed tombs were discovered in structure 22.

Like other buildings in Tulum, the Palace of Halach Uinik was built on a raised platform and the entrance is composed of four columns and a square pillar and contains a roofed shrine in one of the back corridors. It does, however, have certain individual features. The shrine is built against a dividing wall rather than against the back wall and is entered directly through the central door of the portico. The rooms are larger than in any other building in Tulum since it originally contained no columns. However, a column and square pillar had to be built at a later date to support the roof when it began to sag.

The whole of the eastern side is occupied by another roof with an entrace-way of columns. The facade was almost certainly decorated with stucco figures although today all that remains is a sculpture at the central inner entrance leading to the shrine, depicting the inevitable Descending God.

House of Halach Uinik.

Portrayal of the Descending God.
House of Halach Uinik.

The Temple of the Descending God displays the typical outward slope of the outer walls.

Temple of the Descending God
(structure 5)

Although there are numerous images of the Descending God in Tulum, this is the only temple which bears his name. The concept of a descending god existed in many Mesoamerican cultures. For instance, he was called Tzontemoc by the Aztecs, representing the setting sun of evening. However, this symbol was not frequently or widely used to depict the god in the Mayan area. He might represent rain or lightning although he very lekely represented the deity of apiculture, the Bee God, whose name was Ah Mucen Cab.

This temple is located at the northern end of the Inner Precinct and is in fairly good repair in spite of the fact that the Mayas caused the walls to slope outwards at a sharper angle than was customary and adhered to the Tulum custom of building inward sloping door jambs. The temple is built over another flat-roofed structure which was filled in before the temple was built over it. The south-facing double doors of the original building were also walled up.

The temple is entered by means of a small, strutted stairway which is, however, out of line with the building as a whole, clearly demonstrating the unfortunate decline suffered by Mayan archi-

tecture during that period. The eastern wall upon which the temple rests was reinforced by filling in the space between the original structure and the neighbouring building (structure 4).

The dome is similar to that in the Castle, shaped like the sihouette of a bottle. Two benches furnish the further end of the temple and between them there is a small window. In place of a frieze, a three-sectioned cornice gives the finishing touches to the building. The cornice is interrupted above the door by a recess containing a depiction of the winged god in an inverted position as though descending from the sky. The figure is of painted stucco.

Both the main facade and the north and southeastern corners were decorated with painted murals. These were reconstructed

*The image of the Descending God
decorating the entrance to the temple.*

by Miguel Angel Fernandez who also copied and reconstructed
those appearing on the eastern wall within the building. The exterior walls were divided into squares delimited by the interlaced
bodies of snakes, each square containing a religious scene. Certain figures have been identified, among them the gods of the
sun, rain and maize. Figures and offerings adorned the lower edge of the cornice while the central band contains rosettes in relief.
The interior paintings depict various deities in scenes of offerings
each edged with a border, the whole symbolizing the night sky in
which the sun, Venus and the stars appear in combination with
interweaving snakes.

House of the Chultun
(structure 20)

This building stands opposite the Temple of the Frescos. Only thirty years ago it was still in good repair. However, the wooden lintels have since given way, causing the roofing to collapse, leaving it in its present condition. A drawing of the building made by Frederick Catherwood during the last century still exists. Its name is to be attributed to the fact that its southeastern corner stands near a *chultun.*

The Mayas had two methods of obtaining fresh water: from the cenotes or natural springs, or from the *chultunes.* This was an underground, bottle-shaped structure of impermeable limestone in which rain water was gathered. When their water-containing capacity deteriorated they were used for human burial or as domestic waste tips.

This building was no doubt the home of some high-ranking official. It consists of a portico with an entrance-wat composed of two columns and a long, spacious inner corridor with a small sanctuary in the centre. A further corridor was added at the northern end with a small communicating door to avoid the necessity of passing through the portico.

The head of a Mayan figure in stucco was placed in the exact centre of the now fallen main facade. Although damaged, the bust has survived. The walls of the first corridor were painted and even today still bear traces of red and black pigment. A recess was sunk into the wall above the entrance to the second corridor and the original stone decoration it contained is visible beneath the stucco figure of the Descending God which was added later.

Temple of the Initial Series
(structure 9)

This temple is located in the south-eastern area if the Inner Precinct. It faces north and the entrance to the single room within has a stone lintel on the outside and another of wood within. A smooth frieze runs around the four sides, edged with a double band below and a single one above. Originally, stucco figures stood on either side of the entrance, although today only the remains of one figure exist. Similar figures also decorated the roof of the entrance and the corners of the building.

The Temple has the familiar domearoof with the lines of the curved surfaces resembling a neckless bottle. Three small windows face east, south and west respectively.

Inside are to be seen the remains of a small altar upon which stele 1 had originally been placed. This is the stele which,

House of the Chultun.

Temple of the Initial Series.

although dating from before the founding of the city, was nonetheless found in Tulum by Stephens and the fragments later taken
by Thomas Gann to the British Museum in London.

House of Columns
(structure 21)

This building has also been called the Great Palace. It stands to the immediate north of the Temple of the Frescos and was certainly the largest dwelling in Tulum. As we see it today, it is an "L" shaped building although the western wing is almost certainly a later addition. It is flat-roofed and has a spacious entrance formed by four columns. However, its most outstanding feature is the outside gallery, the roof of which was supported by a row of columns dividing it into two, forming a large hall. The inner corridor is long and narrow and a small roofed shrine stands against the back wall. The

House of Columns or
Great Palace.

back wall of the shrine juts out from the outside of the northern
facade. This same facade contains two narrow windows which
are repeated in the wall separating the two corridors. The outer
windows are protected by two crossed bars while the inner ones
were covered by curtains, the supports for which are still visible.
The use of curtains was frequent in the Mayan region as well as in
other cities of Mesoamerica. Curtains served instead of doors as
we know them today. The western wing, which may be of a later
date, has a separate entrance with two columns and a narrow do-
or on the north side, with another door leading into the main
body of the building. It consists of two rooms, one square and
the other rectangular. The former contains a central column.

House of the Cenote
(structure 35)

This building, which originates from two different periods, rests on a cave which was originally a cenote. It was initially a two-roomed structure and later a small room was added to the south-west corner. It was entered by means of a stairway leading from the bottom of the cave to the doorway which faces south. When this third room was built, a doorway was opened into the western corridor of the original building and a stairway built around the mouth of the cenote, leading down to the bottom. The structure today consists of four corridors of which the eastern-most has a portico with two columns and contains two benches. A shrine stands in the western corridor and the central room provides a means of communication between the two entrances of the building. The cenote is entered through the south-east room. The cenote used to fill with rain water, but today the water is salty and polluted by bats.

Habitational Platforms
(structures 26 to 33, 37, 38 and 46 to 53)

The almost unbroken line of platforms 26 to 33 occupies the western side of the main street with an access stairway from the street leading to each of them, with a few exceptions. Only 27 and 32 show any signs of superimposed structures. Structure 33 is the largest platform with a north and west-facing parapet, lying to the south of structure 34-37 and 38 have a lateral connection. They are low constructions and show no signs of having served as a foundation for another structure. 55 is similar to 33, while structures 46 to 53 lie further to the south of the Inner Precinct in the south-eastern section of the city, bordering a street which starts at the south-western entrance in the great wall. 46 and 47 have access stairways, though they are, on the whole, similar to structures 26 to 38.

Tombs
(structures 13, 14 and 19)

Structure 13, standing to the south-west of the Inner Precinct is a platform mounted by way of two small stairways. Two tombs, parts of the roofs of which have fallen in, are visible from above.

Structure 14 is located to the south of·the Temple of Frescos. It has a quadrangular floor with no means of access of any kind. Structure 19 is of greater interest in that it contains a tomb with a

House of the Cenote.

cruciform floor. The remains of human bones were found here together with vessels containing animal bones and traces of food, provided to sustain the dead on their journey, such as shark, sea conch, catfish, iguana, lizard, pigeon, turkey, heron and wild boar.

Guard Towers
(structures 55 and 56

These structures were thus identified by Stephens. There are two such buildings, situated on the north and south-western corners of the great wall. They are, in fact, two small temples, each consisting of a single room with an altar on the north side and doors in the eastern, western and southern walls. It would appear that the outer walls were covered with mural paintings. Structure 55 is decorated with a frieze bearing a criss-cross pattern.

Buildings outside the Great Wall
(structures 57 and 59)

Approximately half a kilometre to the north of the Great Wall, in the area in which the civil population lived, there are two small single room buildings, facing the sea, with particularly thick walls, and curved domes. Structure 59 is of particular interest since it is

Temple of the Wind.

the only building in Tulum with an adornment of cresting composed of two superimposed rows of carved triangles. It is possible that a third row existed but, if so, it no longer exists. It is generally believed that these two buildings are the oldest in the ancient city of Tulum.

Temple of the Wind
(structure 45)

The Temple is built on a natural stone prominence, to the north of the small, sandy beach lying to the east of Tulum. The building is entered from the north and has a single chamber. The remains of stone sculptures were found in the domed ceiling. Grains of barley were identified inside the building. Its most interesting feature is its circular base which brings to mind the architecture of other parts of Mesoamerica, especially that of the Central Highlands where they were employed in the building of temples dedicated to Ehecatl, one of the guises of Quetzalcoatl, as god of the wind.

Temple of the Sea.

Temple of the Sea
(structure 54)

The single chamber of the temple looks out over the Caribbean. Wooden beams support a roof of chalk mixed with sea shells and conches. The remains of a small altar are visible inside.

Platform of the Conches
(structure 60)

This is situated to the west of the Temple of the Wind (structure 45) and was discovered during explorations carried out in 1974 and 1975. The platform is mounted by means of a stairway with decorated struts on the western side white the surface of the platform on the eastern side lies level with the ground. It was given this name on account of the fact that a large number of sea conches were found in its immediate vicinity when the platform was first discovered. If another structure was built on top of it, no traces remain today since such a structure would almost certainly have been built with perishable materials.

House of the North west.

House of the North west
(structure 34)

This building stands at the extreme northern end of the main street. It has a portico with two columns and is entered by means of a westward-facing stairway bordered by struts. It contains two corridors, in the second of which we see a shrine and a very narrow entrance door.

Ceremonial Platforms
(structures 8 and 17)

Such platforms were built in the centre of the city's major squares. We have already mentioned structure 8 which is located in the centre of the Inner Precinct. No. 17 stands to the east of the House of the Frescos and to the south of the House of Columns (structures 15 and 21). The platforms are raised quadrangular structures, each with two symmetrical means of access. structure 8 has an east-west direction and structure 17 lies north-south. They were doubtless used for offerings, sacrifices, ceremonial dances and plays.

Shrines
(structure 15)

This structure is located between the Temple of the Frescos and the House of the Chultun. It is, in fact, a small platform next to which was found stele 2 of Tulum, broken into three pieces.

The stele now stands on a platform where it is supposed to have originally been placed. The stele is marked with a faint hieroglyphic inscription which is too time-worn to be able to identify the date with precision.

(structure 18)

This stands between structures 17 and 21 (House of Columns). All that remains of this structure is a stone block.

(structure 24)

This is a small shrine to the east of structure 25. All that remains of this structure is a quadrangular base with a stairway of four steps facing west.

(structure 36)

This building lies to the north of the House of the Cenote. A small shrine stands opposite the entrance. There is a stairway on its western side and a rectangular cornice runs around the entire building.

The archaeological site also contains numerous other remains of shrines and small temples (structures 39 to 44) in varying states of repair.

GLOSSARY

Arch. Curved construction between two walls, columns, pillars or supports.

Architrave. The lowermost part of an entablature, resting directly on top of the capital of a column.

Bacabs. Mythological Mayan beings whose function was to uphold the four cardinal points upon which the heavens rested.

Balustrade. Structure serving as a border along the sides of a stairway.

Basamento. The part formed by the base and pedestal of a column.

Beam or rafter. A long, thick wooden beam.

Capital. The top part, or head, or a column or pillar, having different kinds of decorative figures, according to the architectural style to which it belongs.

Cenote. A sort of natural well opening into a subterranean stream caused by the sinking of the covering limestone strata of the Yucatan peninsula.

Ceramics. The art of making vessels and other objects out of clay; all kinds of pottery or porcelain; all such objects in general.

Chac. The Maya god of rain.

Chac-Mool. A semi-recumbent sculptured figure with bent knees and inclined head, which some archaeologists define as the representation of the divine messenger between men and the goods.

Chen. A Maya word meaning "well".

Chenes. A Maya style of architecture.

Chontal. Present day name of the Putun group.

Chontalli. Mayan word meaning foreigner.

Chultun. A Maya word meaning "cistern".

Codex. Ancient manuscript of historic or literary importance. Strictly speaking, codices are only those manuscripts that predate the invention of printing. In the Maya culture, only three codices are known to have survived destruction down through the centuries: The *Dresden Codex,* the *Peresian Codex* and the *Tro-Cortesian Codex.*

Column. A supporting pillar consisting of a base, a cylindrical shaft, and a capital, whose purpose is to support roofs or other parts of a structure, or as decoration of buildings.

Colonnade. A group of columns.

Cornice. A horizontal molded projection that crowns or

completes a building or wall. The uppermost part of an entablature. The molding at the top of the walls of a room, between the walls and ceiling.

Corridor. With rooms on either side.

Cresting. An ornamental ridge, as on top of a wall or roof.

Dzonot. A Maya word meaning "well".

Entablature. Group of moldings that crown an architectural structure.

Facade. The exterior face or front part of a building.

Face or surface (of a wall). Either of the two faces of a wall.

Fretwork or fret. An ornamental desing contained within a band or border, consisting of repeated, symmetrical and often geometrical figures.

Frieze. A horizontal part of an entablature between the architrave and cornice. Any decorative horizontal band, as along the upper part of a wall in a room.

Glyph. A decorative grooved figure, engraved or corved in stone.

Haab. Maya Lot calendar of 365 days and fraction.

High relief. A sculptured relief in which the modeled forms project from the background by at least half their depth.

Jade. A very hard and durable mineral stone, usually light green in color, made of magnesium silicate and lime many Stone Age tools were made of this material.

Jamb. The two vertical pieces that support the lintel or arch of doors or windows.

Kukulcan. The Maya name for Quetzalcóatl.

Large mask. A fantastic ornament used as a decorative element in certain architectural works.

Latticework or lattice. An open framework or screen placed over windows or other openings in such a way that persons inside can see without being seen. Used as a decorative element in architecture.

Lintel; Upper part of doors, windows and other openings, resting on the jambs.

Little drum. A semi-circular architectural embellishment.

Low reliev. Sculptural relief projecting very little from the background.

Masonry. Stonework or brickwork made with mortar and irregular stones or blocks.

Mayan arch. A false arch composed of superimposed, layers of stone in which the upper layers project out farther than the lower, and with a horizontal slab on the vortex. It is not as stable as the Roman arch, and was used solely for decorative purposes.

Merlon. The solid portion of a crenelated upper part of a wall or fortress. Also used as a decorative element in some buildings.

Molding. An embellishment in strip form used to decorate buildings or surfaces in architecture or carpentry.

Opening (as for a door). Part of a wall where there is no support for the roof, such as the openings for windows and doors and between columns.

Panel. A flat, usually rectangular piece forming a part of a surface in which it is set, and being raised, recessed, or framed.

Pilaster. Square column or buttress.

Portico. A porch, vestibule or walkway with a roof suported by columns, ofthen leading to the entrance of temples and other sumptuous edifices; a gallery with arcades or columns along a facade or patio.

Popol Vuh. Also called Book of the Council. The sacred book of the Mayas and Quichés, based on oral traditions, known through a version dating from 1534-1539.

Putun. Ancient Mayan group.

Puuc. A maya word meaning "mountain range". Name given to an architectural style.

Quetzal. A beautiful colored bird, it lives in the South Mexico jungle and Central America.

Quetzalcóatl. Plumed serpent, bird serpent, quetzalserpent. Originally a Toltec deity, later venerated throughout Middle America. The creator god of the Fifth Sun, the wind (Ehecatl) and the new race of man. Preaching a religion of love, he taught peoples agriculture, metalwork and the use of the calendar; he established ceremonies and set dates for ceremonies and sacrifices; he proscribed human sacrifices. He furnished man with the means for measuring time and for studying the movements of heavenly bodies.

Rosette. A circular-shaped adornment with various carved motifs.

Sanctuary or shrine. A sacred place or temple where the image or relic of a god is worshipped.

Scabé. A Maya word meaning "white road"

Shaft. The main body of a column, between the base and the capital.

Solid wall. Wall without apertures or openings; in architecture, the part of a wall between two openings.

Square adornment. A square-shaped, projecting architectural embellishment. At times it is carved with various decorative motifs.

Stele or stela. An upright stone or slab with an inscribed or sculptured surface, used as a monument or as a commemorative tablet.

Stucco. A mixture of cement, sand and lime, applied wet and forming a durable finish for exterior walls.

"Sub". The term usually means "beneath".

Tablero. A projecting decorative surface in some parts a building; the flat upper part of the capital.

Talus. The sloping surface or face of a wall or land.

Tzolk'in. A ritual Maya calendar of 260 days.

Vaul or vauting. Unsupported roof, generally made of cuneiform stones. The structure of the vault is supported by walls, pilasters. etc.

Zama. Ancient name of Tulum meaning dawn.

Printed by:
Litoarte, S. de R.L.
F.F. C.C. de Cuernavaca, 683
México 17, D.F.
5000 copies
México City, July, 1982